Get your C

Wild Game & Fish Cookbook: From Deer to
Duck, Goat to Grouse More

BY

Christina Tosch

Copyright Notes

Table of Contents

Introduction

Are you wild about game? Read on and discover the Wild Game Cookbook.

But before you enjoy these 40 recipes guaranteed to please all lovers of wild game everywhere here are 12 facts to inspire you to go wild in the kitchen!

- Grouse is considered to the be the king of all the feathered wild game, the grouse shooting season begins on August 12 which is called the Glorious Twelfth

- The majority of wild game, including farm-raised has a fat content of less than 10 percent, in comparison to well-marbled beef which is can be as high at 40 percent
- Wild salmon is less likely than farm-raised salmon to contain contaminants such as carcinogenic dioxins
- Animals hunted in the wild tender to be a better meat source, largely because they are free-ranging and eat a natural diet
- You can hear a wild turkey's gobble from up to 1 mile away
- Make sure that any fresh wild game you cook reaches an internal temperature of 160 degrees F, while game birds should come in at 165 degrees F
- The wild game in this cookbook fall into four categories: Small game including rabbit, squirrel, frog and beaver. Large wild game such as elk, bear and gator followed by poultry such as goose, duck and wild turkey. There is also a section featuring wild fish recipes.
- Studies reveal that women are more likely to order alligator in a restaurant than men

- Tuna is one of the healthiest wild fish you can eat
- Squirrel meat is the perfect wild game for slow cooking and is a great wild game ingredient for stew
- October is National Hunting and Fishing Month
- During the late 19th century, the traditional bird of choice was goose rather than turkey

Now is the time to get your game on and check out the best-ever 40 recipes in this Wild Game Cookbook.

Fish

Bacon-Wrapped Perch over Coals

This bacon-wrapped perch is the perfect fish to bring the taste of the sea to your very own backyard BBQ. Cooked properly, its skin should be crisp and tasty.

Servings: 4

Total Time: 25mins

Ingredients:

- 1 pound skin-on perch fillets (cleaned)
- ½ tsp pepper
- Freshly squeezed juice of ½ lemon
- 7 ounces bacon
- 1 cup cherry tomatoes (halved)
- Avocado oil

Directions:

1. Preheat your charcoal BBQ to moderate heat.

2. Season the perch with pepper and fresh lemon juice.

3. Wrap each fish fillet in a slice of bacon, adding 2 cherry tomatoes halves inside each one.

4. Lay the fish parcels in a fish basket greased with avocado oil.

5. Place the perch on indirect heat for between 8-10 minutes on each side. (Move the charcoals to one side and lay the fish on the opposite side for indirect heat).

6. Serve with a sprinkle of lemon juice.

Catfish Parmesan

North America boasts literally thousands of rivers and lakes that produce an enormous amount of catfish, some of which are huge. So it stands to reason that there are lots of different recipes out there for this freshwater fish. And one of the best ways to serve catfish is crusted.

Servings: 6

Total Time: 35mins

Ingredients:

- ¾ cup dry breadcrumbs
- 3 tbsp Parmesan cheese (grated)
- 2 tbsp fresh parsley (chopped)
- ½ tsp salt
- ¼ tsp paprika
- ⅛ tsp pepper
- ⅛ tsp dried oregano
- ⅛ tsp basil
- 6 (4 ounce) catfish fillets
- ½ cup butter (melted)
- Tartar sauce (to serve)

Directions:

1. In a bowl, combine the breadcrumbs with the Parmesan cheese, parsley, salt, paprika, pepper, oregano, and basil.

2. Dip the fish first in the melted butter and second in the Parmesan crumb mixture.

3. Place the fish in a greased 13x9" casserole dish.

4. Bake in the oven, uncovered at 375 degrees F. for 20-25 minutes, until the fish flakes easily when using a fork.

5. Serve with a dollop of tartar sauce.

Lime and Basil Grilled Swordfish Steaks

This mild-tasting, white-fleshed fish has a meaty texture and is a good choice for anyone who isn't a full-on fish lover.

Servings: 4

Total Time: 35mins

Ingredients:

- ¼ cup olive oil
- 2 tbsp fresh lime juice
- 1 tbsp fresh basil (chopped)
- 1 clove garlic (peeled, minced)
- ½ tsp salt
- ¼ tsp black pepper
- 4 (6 ounces, 1" thick) swordfish steaks

Directions:

1. In an extra large-size resealable bag, combine the oil with the fresh lime juice, fresh basil, garlic salt, and black pepper.

2. Add the fish and coast the fish evenly with the marinade. Set aside to rest for 15 minutes.

3. In the meantime, preheat the grill.

4. Over moderately high heat grill the fish for approximately 4-5 minutes on each side, or until the fish is entirely cooked through.

5. Serve with your favorite grilled veggies.

Marlin Burgers

Marlin has a firm and almost steak-like flavor, which makes it the perfect fish for patties. Serve with a crisp green salad.

Servings: 4

Total Time: 50mins

Ingredients:

- 1¼ pounds marlin tuna
- 1 cup breadcrumbs
- 1 medium-size egg
- 1 onion (peeled, finely chopped)
- 1 tbsp ginger (peeled, finely grated)
- 2 tsp garlic (peeled, finely grated)
- 2 tbsp mayonnaise
- 4 tsp olive oil
- 1 tsp toasted sesame oil
- Kosher salt
- Freshly ground black pepper
- Green salad (to serve, optional)

Directions:

1. Chill the marlin in the freezer until firm.

2. Chill your grinder blade in the freezer for 15 minutes.

3. Assemble the grinder attachment and put a large mixing bowl alongside it to catch the ground fish flesh.

4. Grind the fish. Alternatively, pulse the fish in a food processor, while taking care not to allow the flesh to become mushy.

5. In a large-size bowl, combine the fish with the breadcrumbs, egg, onion, ginger, and garlic.

6. Stir in the mayonnaise, olive oil, and sesame oil.

7. Form the mixture into small-size patties.

8. Season some salt and black pepper in the patties

9. Pan-fry or grill the patties over moderate heat for 3-4 minutes per side,

until just cooked through.

Pike Chili

Banish the beef and pass on the pork, instead opt for a chili made with fresh fish. It works equally as well as red meat and what's more, it's far healthier.

Servings: 4

Total Time: 25mins

Ingredients:

- 1 tbsp olive oil
- ½ cup red pepper (diced)
- 2 garlic cloves (peeled, minced)
- ½ cup onion (peeled, chopped)
- 2 (14 ounce) cans crushed tomatoes
- 1 (14 ounces) kidney bean (drained)
- 2 tbsp cornstarch
- ¼ cup water
- 2 tbsp parsley
- 1 tsp chili powder
- ⅛tsp cayenne pepper
- 1 pound northern pike fillets (cut into 1" cubes)

Directions:

1. In a pan, heat the oil.

2. Add the red pepper along with the garlic and onion, sauté until gently brown.

3. Add the crushed tomatoes, kidney beans, cornstarch, water, parsley, chili powder, and cayenne pepper.

4. Cover the pan and simmer while occasionally stirring until the mixture starts to thicken.

5. Add the pike to the pan and simmer for 10 minutes, until the fish is entirely cooked.

6. Serve the chili with rice and chunks of bread.

Salsa Fish

Rich in vitamins and protein, bass is quite low in calories. Sea bass is mild in flavor, and its white meat is tender but firm. It is perfect for cooking as it doesn't fall apart as easily as flaky fish.

Servings: 6

Total Time: 15mins

Ingredients:

- 2 pounds bass fillets
- 1 cup seasoned breadcrumbs
- 1 tbsp vegetable oil
- 1½ cups salsa
- 8 ounces partly-skimmed mozzarella cheese (shredded)

Directions:

1. Coat the bass in breadcrumbs.

2. In a frying pan, brown the fish in the oil.

3. Arrange the fish in a greased 13x9" casserole dish.

4. Top with the salsa and the shredded cheese.

5. Bake in the oven, uncovered, at 400 degrees F, for 8-10 minutes, until the fish flakes easily when using a fork, and the cheese is entirely melted.

Spicy Blackened Redfish

Redfish live in the Gulf of Mexico, Atlantic Ocean, Texas, and Louisiana. Small redfish weighing less than around 15 pounds have a sweet, mild flavor, and their white meat is moist and tasty.

Servings: 6

Total Time: 1hour

Ingredients

- 2½ tsp salt
- 1 tsp onion powder
- 1 tsp cayenne pepper
- 1 tsp garlic powder
- ¾ tsp freshly ground black pepper
- ¾ tsp freshly ground white pepper
- 12 ounces butter (melted)
- 6 (8 ounces, ½" thick) boneless, skinless filets redfish
- ½ tsp dried thyme
- ½ tsp dried oregano

Directions:

1. In a bowl, combine the paprika with the salt, onion powder, cayenne, garlic powder, black pepper, and white pepper. Set to one side.

2. Add 2 tablespoons of butter each into 6 small-size ramekins. Put to one side and keep warm.

3. Put the remaining butter in a wide but shallow bowl.

4. Dip each fish fillet in the butter and lay on a baking tray lined with parchment paper.

5. Liberally dust each fish fillet on both sides with the spices mixture, gently pressing into is flesh. Sprinkle with thyme and oregano, and again press into the fish using clean hands.

6. Pour the remaining melted butter into a small-size bowl.

7. Preheat the main oven to 200 degrees F.

8. Over high heat, heat a large frying pan for 8-10 minutes, until white and ashy (you may want to open the windows or turn on the ventilation fan at this stage).

9. Place 2-3 fish fillets in the pan, standing as far back as possible to avoid any unpleasant smoke.

10. Pour 1 teaspoon of the remaining melted butter over each of the fillets.

11. Cook the fish until the underside of each fish is charred, this will take approximately 2 minutes.

12. Flip the fish over and pour 1 teaspoon of melted butter over each one.

13. Continue to cook until the fish is sufficiently cooked through.

14. Transfer the fish to a cooking rack and keep warm in the oven.

15. Repeat until all filets are cooked.

16. Serve and enjoy.

Spicy Plum Salmon

Plums are a refreshing contrast in texture and flavor to juicy, moist grilled salmon.

Servings: 6

Total Time: 35mins

Ingredients:

- 5 medium-size plums (divided)
- ½ cup water
- 1 chipotle pepper in adobo sauce (finely chopped)
- 2 tbsp ketchup
- 1 tbsp sugar
- 1 tbsp olive oil
- 6 (6 ounce) wild salmon fillets
- ¾ tsp salt

Directions:

1. Coarsely chop and pit 2 plums and add them to a pan.

2. Add the water and bring to boil before reducing the heat to a simmer, while uncovered for approximately 10-15 minutes, until the plums are soft and the liquid is almost entirely evaporated.

3. Set aside to slightly cool before transferring to a food blender.

4. Add the ketchup followed by the chipotle, sugar, and olive oil.

5. Process in the blender until a puree. Set ¾ cup aside for serving.

6. Season the fish with salt, and place on a greased grill rack, skin side facing upwards.

7. Grill, while covered, over moderate heat until the fish is beginning to easily flake with a fork, for approximately 10 minutes.

8. Brush the fish with the remaining sauce during the final few minutes of cooking.

9. Slice and pit the remaining plums and serve the fish with the slices of plums.

Trout Baked in Cream

Oregon has many different types of fishing, but trout is the number one game fish, and this recipe perfectly showcases its mild and delicate flavor.

Servings: 4-6

Total Time: 20mins

Ingredients:

- 6 (4 ounce) trout fillets
- 2 tbsp fresh lemon juice
- 1 tsp dill weed
- ½ tsp salt
- ⅛ tsp black pepper
- 1 cup heavy whipping cream
- 2 tbsp seasoned breadcrumbs

Directions:

1. Arrange the trout in a greased 13x9" casserole dish.

2. Sprinkle with fresh lemon juice, dill weeds, salt, and black pepper.

3. Pour the heavy whipping cream over the fish and scatter with breadcrumbs.

4. Bake at 350 degrees F in the oven, uncovered for 12-15 minutes, until the fish flakes easily with a fork.

Wicked Tuna Fettuccine

Fresh tuna is way better than its canned counterpart. Not only is it delicious, but also it is higher in fatty acids.

Servings: 2

Total Time: 1hour 40mins

Ingredients:

- 8 tbsp white wine (divided)
- 3 tbsp olive oil (divided)
- 1 tsp dried oregano (divided)
- 1 tsp dried basil (divided)
- ¼ tsp salt (divided)
- ⅛ tsp black pepper (divided)
- 1 (10 ounce) tuna steak (cut in half)
- ½ cup sweet onion (thinly sliced)
- 1 cup canned diced tomatoes (undrained)
- ¼ tsp brown sugar
- 3 ounces uncooked fettuccine

Directions:

1. In a bowl, combine 2 tablespoons of white wine with 2 tablespoons of oil, ¼ teaspoon of oregano and basil, half of the salt, and black pepper. Add the tuna steak, turn to evenly coat, cover with a lid, and transfer to the fridge for 60 minutes.

2. In a frying pan, sauté the onion in the remaining olive oil until fork tender.

3. Add the tomatoes along with the brown sugar and remaining white wine, oregano, basil, salt, and black pepper.

4. Bring to boil before turning the heat down to a simmer, and simmer while uncovered for 4-6 minutes, until slightly thickened and bubbly.

5. Meanwhile, keep cooking the pasta according to the package instructions.

6. Drain the tuna steaks and discard the marinade.

7. Arrange the tuna over the tomato mixture. Return to the boil.

8. Turn the heat down, and covered, simmer for approximately 6 minutes, until the fish easily flakes with a fork.

9. Remove the tuna and keep warm.

10. Unload the pasta and add it to the tomato mixture, tossing to coat.

11. Divide between 2 bowls and top with tuna.

Large Game

Bison Fajitas

Bison or to give it its other name North American Buffalo is even better than beef. It has fewer calories and less fat. It's also a good source of iron, B-vitamins, and more.

Servings: 10-12

Total Time: 6hours 40mins

Ingredients:

Marinade:

- ¼ cup tequila
- 2 tbsp fresh cilantro (chopped)
- 4 garlic cloves (peeled, finely chopped)
- ½ tsp grated lime peel (grated)
- 1 tbsp freshly squeezed fresh lime juice
- ½ tsp red pepper flakes
- ½ tsp salt
- ¼ tsp ground black pepper

Fajitas:

- 1½ pounds bison flank steak (cut into 1" strips)
- 1 tbsp cooking oil
- 1 medium-size onion (peeled, thinly sliced)
- ½ medium-size green bell pepper (thinly sliced into strips)
- ½ medium-size red bell pepper (thinly sliced into strips)
- ½ medium-size yellow bell pepper (thinly sliced into strips)
- ⅔ cup tomato (chopped)
- 3 large red cayenne peppers chopped (stemmed, seeded)
- 12 flour tortillas (warm)

To Serve:

- Sour cream
- Store-bought guacamole
- Cheese (shredded)
- Store-bought salsa

Directions:

1. Combine the tequila with the cilantro, garlic, lime peel, lime juice, red pepper flakes, salt, and pepper in a ziplock bag.

2. Add the strips of bison to the bag, seal the bag, and gently turn to coat evenly. Transfer to the fridge for 6-24 hours.

3. Pour the oil into a large-size frying pan and cook the onion along with the peppers until crisp-tender.

4. Remove from the pan and add half of the undrained strips of bison to the hot pan. Cook for between 2-3 minutes, depending on your preferred level of doneness.

5. Repeat with the remaining strips of meat.

6. Bring the veggies to the pan and add the tomatoes along with the hot peppers.

7. Cook, while stirring for about 1-2 minutes, or until sufficiently heated through.

8. Warm the tortillas.

9. To assemble, fill the warmed tortilla with the mixture.

10. Serve with prepared dollop of sour cream and guacamole.

11. Scatter with cheese and add a spoonful of salsa.

Cajun Coyote

Coyote meat, so says dedicated hunters tastes a lot like beef. It's tender and tasty, so if you are feeling adventurous, this recipe is the one for you.

Servings: 6-8

Total Time: 45mins

Ingredients:

- 2 cups vegetable oil
- 2 tbsp dried Italian seasoning
- 2 tbsp Cajun seasoning
- 2 tbsp lemon pepper
- Garlic powder (to taste)
- 2 pounds coyote meat (pounded to ½ "thickness)

Directions:

1. In a large-size shallow dish, combine the oil with the Italian and Cajun seasonings, lemon pepper and garlic powder.

2. Lay the meat in the dish, turning to coat with the seasoning mixture evenly.

3. Cover and place in the fridge for 30 minutes.

4. Preheat your broiler for high heat.

5. Light oil the grill grate.

6. Unload and discard the marinade from the meat.

7. Place the meat on the hot grill and cook until the meat is cooked through and its juices run entirely clear, this will take between 6-8 minutes.

Elk and Roasted Garlic Sandwiches

Neither gamey nor tough, this lean meat is perfect for shredding and using as a sandwich filling alternative to pork. What's also good news is that 3 ounce serving of elk is approximately only 165 calories.

Servings: 8-10

Total Time: 8hours 50mins

Ingredients:

- ½ head of roasted garlic
- Oil
- 1 tsp salt
- 1 tsp freshly ground black pepper
- 1 tsp smoked paprika
- 1½ tsp onion powder
- 2½ pounds elk roast
- ¼ cup loosely packed brown sugar
- ½ cup beer
- ¼ cup blueberries
- Buns (split, and toasted, to serve)
- Barbecue sauce (store-bought, to serve)

Directions:

1. Set the main oven to 400 degrees F.

2. To roast the garlic: Trim the top off the garlic bulb, approximately ¼ ".

3. Peel away the paper skin.

4. Drizzle with oil and set aside for 60 seconds.

5. Wrap the garlic in foil and place in the oven for 45-60 minutes. The bulb is ready when the tops of the cloves are golden.

6. Set aside to slightly cook before gently squeezing the cloves out of the skin.

7. Mash and use as directed.

8. For the sandwiches: Add the meat to a crockpot.

9. Sprinkle the salt, black pepper, paprika, and onion powder over the elk roast.

10. Tip the brown sugar over the roast.

11. Pour the beer over the sugar and scatter with blueberries.

12. On low heat, cook for 7-8 hours.

13. Using 2 forks finely shred the meat. Add the roasted garlic to fully combine with the meat and cook for an additional 30 minutes.

14. Transfer the roast to a baking sheet lined with aluminum foil and cook at 400 degrees F for 10-15 minutes until the ends begin to crisp.

15. Transfer the meat to the crockpot and stir well with the remaining juice.

16. Toast the buns, pile the meat on top, and drizzle with your favorite barbecue sauce.

17. Enjoy.

Gator Gumbo

N'Awlins gumbo kicks-up a gear with some big game, gator.

Servings: 8-10

Total Time: 1hour 30mins

Ingredients:

- ½ cup green onions (chopped)
- 3 cloves garlic (peeled, minced)
- ½ cup red bell pepper (seeded, chopped)
- ½ cup green bell pepper (seeded, chopped)
- ¼ cup parsley (chopped)
- 4 stalks celery (chopped)
- 2 (28 ounce) large cans stewed tomatoes
- 1 tsp ground cayenne pepper
- 1 tsp ground black pepper
- ½ tsp salt (to taste)
- 2 pounds cooked and stemmed okra + cooking liquid
- 2 pounds gator meat (cut into 1" long, ¼" thick strips)
- Rice (to serve, optional)
- Hot buttered cornbread (to serve, optional)

Directions:

1. In a pan, sauté the onions, garlic, red and green peppers until softened.

2. Add the parsley, celery, stewed tomatoes, cayenne pepper, black pepper, and salt, and simmer for 10 minutes, in a large, covered pot.

3. Add the cooked okra to the pot along with some of its liquid and cook for an additional 10 minutes.

4. Add the gator mat and over low heat cook for approximately 60 minutes, until tender. You may, at this point, need to add a drop hotter water to thin the gravy out.

5. Serve the gumbo on a bed of rice with a side of hot buttered cornbread.

Goat Chops in Red Wine

Here is your opportunity to discover why goat meat accounts for approximately 6 percent of the world's red meat consumption.

Servings: 4

Total Time: 45mins

Ingredients:

- 1 clove of garlic (peeled)
- ⅔ cup red wine
- Pinch of dried chili flakes
- 8 goat chops
- Black pepper (to season)

Directions:

1. Preheat your grill to high heat.

2. Add the garlic, red wine, and chili flakes to a shallow bowl.

3. Place the chops in the marinade and set aside at room temperature for 30 minutes.

4. Take the chops out of the marinade, gently shaking to remove any excess marinade.

5. Place the goat chops on the preheated grill and cook for 4-5 minutes on each side. They are sufficiently cooked to medium-rare doneness when they register an internal temperature of 145 degrees F.

6. Take the chops out of the grill and set aside to rest for a few minutes before serving.

Grilled Black Bear Tenderloin

Bear tastes sweeter than venison and is redder in color than beef. The golden rule to successfully grilling black bear is to remove all of the fat. This step prevents the fat from igniting!

Servings: 4

Total Time: 35mins

Ingredients:

- 1 tsp salt
- 1½ tsp black pepper
- 1½ tsp ground allspice
- ¾ tsp ground cloves
- ¾ tsp ground cinnamon
- ½ tsp ground nutmeg
- Oil (as needed)
- 1 pound bear tenderloin (all fat and silver skin removed)

Directions:

1. In a bowl, combine the salt with the black pepper, allspice, cloves, cinnamon and nutmeg.

2. Add oil to the mix to create a paste.

3. Rub all sides of the bear meat with the spice paste. Put to one side.

4. Preheat your charcoal grill for moderate heat.

5. Put the bear tenderloin on the grill and slowly cook on moderate heat (375 degrees F) until the meat becomes an internal temperature of 160 degrees F. You will need to occasionally turn the meat over during the cooking process. As a guide, allow 20-25 minutes per pound.

6. Take out of the grill and allow to cool for 3 minutes before serving.

Spicy Apricot-Bourbon Wild Turkey

Wild turkey is one of the tastiest game meats around and this recipe combines tart BBQ sauce with sweet apricot jam to deliver a really satisfying dish. Serve with creamy mash for the ultimate family meal.

Servings: 4

Total Time: 3hours 15mins

Ingredients:

- 4 skinless, wild turkey thighs
- Kosher salt
- Freshly cracked black pepper
- 2 tbsp olive oil
- 1 large-size onion (peeled, chopped)
- 2 tbsp butter
- 1 tsp fresh thyme leaves
- 1 bay leaf
- 4 garlic cloves (peeled, minced)
- ¾ cup bourbon
- 2 cups tart, store-bought BBQ sauce
- ¾ cup apricot jam
- ¼ cup water
- ¼ tsp cayenne pepper
- 1 tsp Worcestershire sauce
- 1 tbsp coarsely-ground mustard
- Mash potatoes (to serve, optional)
- Fresh chives (chopped, to garnish)

Directions:

1. Preheat the main oven to 300 degrees F.

2. Using kitchen paper, pat the turkey thigh dry and season well with salt and pepper.

3. Over moderate-high heat, in a pot, heat 2 tablespoons of oil.

4. Brown the turkey thighs on both sides and transfer to a casserole dish. Set the dish to one side.

5. Reduce the heat to moderate and

6. Add the onion and butter to the pot. Sweat while constantly stirring until the onions are gently browned and translucent,

7. Next, add the thyme, bay leaf, and garlic and continue stirring for 30 seconds.

8. Pour in the bourbon and reduce, while scraping the bottom of the pan with a wooden spoon, until the mixture is almost evaporated.

9. Add the BBQ sauce, apricot jam, water, cayenne, Worcestershire sauce, and mustard and whisk to entire combine.

10. Return the now browned turkey to the pot, cover with aluminum foil and close with the lid. This will help to slow down any loss of moisture.

11. Transfer the pot to the oven and bake at 300 degrees F for 3-4 hours, until the turkey is tender. You will need to flip the thighs over halfway through cooking.

12. Serve the turkey over mashed potatoes and garnish with chopped chives.

Swedish-Style Moose Meatballs

Moose meat is dense, which makes it ideal for meatballs. It has a strong gamey taste, and in this recipe, allspice is the star of the show. Serve over egg noodles and enjoy meatballs with a difference.

Servings: 2-4

Total Time: 50mins

Ingredients:

- 1 pound ground moose meat
- ½ cup breadcrumbs
- ½ cup + ¼ cup milk (divided)
- 1 large-size egg
- 2 garlic cloves (peeled)
- ⅛ tsp allspice
- Salt and black pepper
- 1 tbsp olive oil
- 1½ tbsp butter
- 1½ tbsp all-purpose flour
- 1 cup beef broth
- 8 ounces egg noodles

Directions:

1. Using clean hands, in a bowl, combine the moose meat with the breadcrumbs, ¼ cup milk, egg, garlic, allspice, salt, and pepper. Mix well to combine. It may be necessary to add more breadcrumbs if the mixture is too soft.

2. With a small-size ice cream scoop, make the mixture into evenly-sized balls.

3. Fry the meatballs in 1 tablespoon of oil, until medium-rare.

4. In a pan, melt the butter.

5. Add the flour to the melted butter and stir to create a roux.

6. On low heat, cook the roux for 5 minutes.

7. Add ¾ cup of beef broth to the roux and stir until it bubbles.

8. Continue stirring while adding the remaining ½ cup of milk.

9. Over low heat, simmer until the sauce starts to bubble. Taste and season. You can thin the sauce add by adding the remaining broth.

10. Add the meatballs to the sauce, leaving the fat in the pan.

11. Keep the meatballs and sauce warm over low heat.

12. Cook the egg noodles according to the package instructions until al dent, for 5-7 minutes. Drain.

13. Transfer the noodles to individual bowl and top with the meatballs and sauce.

14. Serve and enjoy.

Venison Pot Roast with Mixed Vegetables

This venison pot roast is a great way to showcase this lean game meat.

Servings: 6-8

Total Time: 3hours 15mins

Ingredients:

- 3 tbsp all-purpose flour
- ½ tsp salt
- ½ tsp pepper
- 1 medium-size onion (peeled, sliced)
- 1 (3-4 pound) boneless venison roast
- 2 tbsp canola oil
- 1 cup apple cider
- 1 cup beef broth
- 1 tsp dried thyme
- 1 bay leaf
- 8 small-size potatoes (peeled)
- 6 medium-size carrots (cut into 2" pieces)
- 4 celery ribs (cut into 2" pieces)

Directions:

1. Combine the flour with the salt and pepper and rub the mixture all over the venison roast.

2. In a 12" Dutch oven, brown the onions in oil until softened, add the meat and brown on all sides.

3. Pour in the apple cider and broth and add the thyme and bay leaf.

4. Bring the mixture to boil before reducing the heat.

5. Cover and simmer for 2 hours.

6. Next, add the potatoes, followed by the carrots and celery.

7. Cover and simmer for 60 minutes until the meat and veggies are tender.

8. Remove and discard the bay leaf.

9. Enjoy.

Wild Boar in Dry Red Wine

If you are a newbie to cooking game, then wild boar may sound a bit intimidating, but that really isn't the case with this simple recipe.

Servings: 4

Total Time: 3hours

Ingredients:

- 2½ pounds wild boar (washed, patted dry)
- 1 cup olive oil
- 5 sprigs fresh rosemary
- 5 garlic cloves (peeled, crushed)
- 5 juniper seeds
- 20 green beans
- 10 baby carrots
- 2 large-size pears (cored, sliced)
- 16 wild mushrooms
- 5 slices of bacon

Sauce:

- 8 ounces dry red wine
- 1 tsp sugar
- 1 pork bouillon cube

Directions:

1. Place the meat in an ovenproof dish.

2. Pour the oil over the meat and add the rosemary, garlic, and juniper seeds.

3. Transfer to the fridge to marinate for 60 minutes.

4. Preheat the main oven to 190 degrees F.

5. Remove the boar from the marinade and cook in the preheated oven for approximately 90 minutes.

6. In a pan, lightly boil the green beans along with the carrots. Drain.

7. Half an hour before cooking the meat, add the carrots to the ovenproof dish along with the pear slices and mushrooms.

8. Wrap 4 green beans with a slice of bacon and add to the ovenproof dish 15 minutes before the meat is cooked through.

9. Transfer the meat to a warm plate. Slice.

10. Arrange the baby carrots, slices of pear, and wild mushrooms around the meat.

11. Discard the oil and garlic from the ovenproof dish.

12. Add the red wine, sugar, and bouillon cube to the now-empty ovenproof dish, and over moderate heat, slowly heat to reduce.

13. Pour the red wine mixture over the sliced boar and veggies.

14. Serve and enjoy.

Poultry

Baked Pheasant with Gravy

A simple and hearty meal, the ideal comfort food, pheasant is a gamey meat and makes for a tasty main meal when marinated in brown sugar and flour.

Servings: 6

Total Time: 1hour

Ingredients:

- ½ cup brown sugar
- ½ cup all-purpose flour
- 6 pheasant breast halves
- 3 tbsp salted butter
- 1¼ cups water
- 1 (10¾ ounce) can condensed cream of celery soup
- 1 cup chicken stock
- 1 (2.8 ounce) can French-fried onions
- Mashed potato (to serve)

Directions:

1. Set the main oven to 350 degrees F and grease a large baking dish.

2. Combine the brown sugar and flour in a plastic, resealable food bag.

3. One at a time, add the pheasant breast halves to the bag and shake to coat evenly in the mixture.

4. Dissolve the butter in a skillet over moderate heat. Add the pheasant and brown on both sides. Transfer to the baking dish.

5. In a jug, stir together the water, condensed soup, and chicken stock. Pour the mixture over the meat.

6. Bake in the oven for 40 minutes. Scatter the canned onions over the pheasant and then return to the oven for several more minutes until the meat's juices run clear.

7. Serve with mashed potato.

Citrus-Stuffed Christmas Goose

Over the years, goose has been replaced by turkey on the Christmas menu. Here, it makes a welcome return and what better way to celebrate the festive season than with this festive citrus goose?

Servings: 8

Total Time: 2hours 30mins

Ingredients:

- 1 (10-12 pound) goose
- Salt and black pepper
- 1 apple (peeled, quartered)
- 1 orange (peeled, quartered)
- 1 lemon (peeled, quartered)
- 1 cup hot water

Directions:

1. Set the main oven to 350 degrees F

2. Season the goose all over with salt and black pepper, including inside the cavity.

3. Stuff the fruit into the cavity and arrange the bird, breast side up, on a rack inside a roasting tin.

4. Prick the skin several times using a fork and pour water into the bottom of the roasting tin.

5. Leave in the oven and roast for 2½-3 hours until a thermometer registers an internal temperature of 180 degrees F.

6. Take the bird out of the oven, tent loosely with aluminum kitchen foil, and allow to stand for 15 minutes before discarding the fruit, carving, and serving.

Cornish Hens with Chestnut and Cranberry Wild Rice Stuffing

Cranberry, chestnut, celery and wild rice baked inside moist and juicy Cornish hens is a delicious all-in-one meal.

Servings: 10

Total Time: 1hour 15mins

Ingredients:

- Nonstick cooking spray
- 2 tbsp salted butter
- ¼ cup fresh mushrooms (sliced)
- ½ cup celery (chopped)
- 2 (6.2 ounce) packages quick-cook wild rice mix
- Salt and black pepper
- ½ cup water
- 2 (14½ ounce) cans reduced-salt chicken stock
- ½ cup dried cranberries
- ⅔ cup canned sliced water chestnuts (drained, chopped)
- 2 tbsp soy sauce
- ½ cup green onions (chopped)
- 5 (22-24 ounce) Cornish game hens

Directions:

1. Set the main oven to 375 degrees F.

2. Spritz a saucepan with nonstick cooking spray. Apply the butter to the pan and melt over moderate heat.

3. Add the mushrooms and celery, sauté until tender.

4. Stir in the wild rice and cook another 60 seconds, season with salt and black pepper.

5. Pour in the water and broth. Bring the mixture to a boil, then turn down to a simmer and cover with a lid for 5 minutes until the rice is tender.

6. Stir in the cranberries, chestnuts, soy sauce, and green onions until incorporated. Stuff the 5 hens with an equal amount of the rice mixture.

7. Arrange the birds in a roasting pan and bake in the oven for just under an hour or until a meat thermometer registers a temperature of 170 degrees F.

8. To serve, cut each bird in half.

Creamed Squab on Toast

Squab tastes a little like dark chicken. Golden toast provides the perfect base for squab and helps to balance the richness of what is a tasty appetizer.

Servings: 4

Total Time: 1hour 30mins

Ingredients:

- 2 quarts water
- 1 bay leaf
- 4 (1 pound) squab
- 2 tbsp salted butter
- ½ cup fresh mushrooms (sliced)
- ½ cup yellow onion (chopped)
- 2 tbsp all-purpose flour
- 1 cup chicken stock
- 2 tbsp fresh lemon juice
- ½ tsp salt
- ⅛ tsp black pepper
- ¼ cup heavy whipping cream
- 2 tbsp fresh parsley (minced)
- Toasted bread (cut into triangles)
- Fresh parsley (chopped, to garnish)

Directions:

1. In Dutch oven over moderate heat, add the water and bay leaf, bring to a boil and add the squab.

2. Turn down the heat to a simmer, coat, and cook until tender. Take the grouse out of the pot and set aside to cool.

3. Take the meat out of the bones (discard the bones) and chop into small pieces.

4. Tighten the cooking liquid from the pan and set to one side to use later.

5. Dissolve the butter in a skillet over moderate heat, add the mushrooms and onion, sauté until tender.

6. Stir in the flour until incorporated.

7. Pour in the chicken stock, lemon juice, salt, and black pepper. Bring the mixture to a boil for 2 minutes, while stirring, until thickened.

8. Add the grouse to the skillet and cook until hot through.

9. Fold in the heavy cream and fresh parsley. Cook for 60 more seconds before serving over toast garnished with more fresh parsley.

Dove and Fresh Fig Kabobs

The delicate flavor of dove is the perfect complement to sweet juicy figs. They are low in fat, and you can't buy them in a regular store. So, if you have a keen hunter in your family, why not try these gourmet kabobs?

Servings: 8

Total Time: 3hours 20mins

Ingredients:

- ¾ cup teriyaki sauce
- 1 cup red wine
- ¾ cup store-bought BBQ sauce
- 16 dove breasts (carved from the bone)
- 16 fresh figs (halved)

Directions:

1. Combine the teriyaki sauce, red wine, and BBQ sauce in a saucepan over moderate heat and simmer for 10 minutes. Take off the heat and transfer to a bowl.

2. Add the dove breasts to the prepared marinade and allow them to soak for 2-3 hours.

3. Preheat your oven to broil.

4. Skewer the duck breasts and fresh fig halves using either metal or bamboo skewers soaked in water.

5. Place a rack inside a sheet tray and place the kabobs on top.

6. Put in the oven and cook for 10 minutes. Flip the skewers over halfway through cooking.

7. Leave for 5-10 minutes before serving.

Egyptian Pigeon with Freekeh Wheat Salad

Pigeons are low in fat, and their meat is dark. They are nutritious and delicious, and this pigeon recipe is flavored with powerful Egyptian spices to create a tasty dish, which is guaranteed to impress.

Servings: 6

Total Time: 45mins

Ingredients:

- 6 pigeons (plucked)
- Olive oil

Spice Rub:

- 2 tsp dried oregano
- 1 tsp each ground cinnamon, cayenne, cumin, coriander, black pepper, cardamom
- ¼ tsp ground cloves
- 1 tsp salt
- 1 tsp dried mint

Freekeh Salad:

- 2 cups poultry broth
- 2 cups freekeh
- 2 tbsp olive oil
- ½ cup shallots (minced)
- 1 red bell pepper (seeded, diced)
- 2 cloves garlic (peeled and minced)
- 3 tbsp extra-virgin olive oil
- Salt and black pepper
- Fresh lemon juice

Directions:

1. Rub the pigeons all over with olive oil.

2. Prepare the spice rub: in a bowl, combine the oregano, cinnamon, cayenne pepper, cumin, coriander, black pepper, cardamom, cloves, salt, and mint.

3. Rub the birds evenly with the spice mixture.

4. Transfer the birds to a resealable container and chill overnight.

5. An hour before you wish to cook the birds, take them out of the refrigerator and allow them to come to room temperature.

6. In the meantime, prepare the salad.

7. In a deep pot, bring the poultry broth to a boil and add the freekeh. Stir and then bring the liquid back to a boil, cover with a lid and turn off the heat. Allow to stand for half an hour.

8. Warm the olive oil in a pan over moderately high heat, then add the shallots and sauté for a few minutes until browned.

9. Add the bell pepper and garlic and sauté for 60 more seconds. Turn off the heat.

10. Preheat an outdoor grill to high heat.

11. When the grill is hot, drop a little more olive oil over the pigeons and place them on the grill, breast side up. Cook for 10 minutes before flipping, you can place a clean brick on top of the pigeon breasts to help them make better contact with the grill. Cook for another 3-5 minutes until cooked with just a little pink on the inside.

12. Take the pigeons off the grill and allow to rest for several minutes.

13. Finish preparing the salad. Add the cooked freekeh to a pan over moderate heat along with the olive oil, salt, black pepper, and some lemon juice. Cook until warm through and serve alongside the pigeon.

Guinea Fowl Tagine with Apricots, Chickpeas, and Squash

Fragrant Moroccan spices bring heat and sweetness to this delicious tagine, which smells almost as delicious as it tastes. Guinea fowl is ideal in a tagine as it is lean, moist, and full of flavor. Its meat is white, and it tastes a little like pheasant but minus the gamey taste.

Servings: 6

Total Time: 1hour 30mins

Ingredients:

- 3 tbsp olive oil
- 2 guinea fowl (jointed)
- Salt and black pepper
- 2 yellow onions (peeled, chopped)
- 2 cloves garlic (peeled, chopped)
- 1 butternut squash (peeled, deseeded, chopped)
- 1 tsp ground coriander
- ¼ tsp ground ginger
- 1 tsp ground cumin
- 1 tbsp ras-el-hanout
- 1 cinnamon stick
- Squeeze honey
- Generous pinch saffron (soaked in 1 tbsp boiling water)
- Juice of 1 medium lemon
- 1 (14 ounce) can chickpeas (drained and rinsed)
- 3⅔ cups chicken broth
- 7 ounces dried apricots
- Small bunch fresh cilantro
- Couscous (to serve)

Directions:

1. Warm the oil in a huge casserole dish or tagine over moderate heat.

2. Season the guinea fowl with salt and black pepper. Brown the guinea fowl in batches in the casserole dish then set to one side.

3. Using the same dish, sauté the onions, garlic, and squash until softened.

4. Stir in the coriander, ginger, cumin, ras-el-hanout, and cinnamon. Allow to cook for 3-4 minutes before squeezing in some honey and adding the soaked saffron and fresh lemon juice.

5. Next, add the chickpeas and chicken broth, stir to combine.

6. Return the guinea fowl to the pot along with the apricots. Cover the dish with a lid and simmer for approximately an hour, until the meat is cooked through and the squash is tender.

7. Decorate with fresh cilantro and serve with couscous.

Partridge in a Pear Tree

If you are tired of turkey, then partridge is an excellent alternative for Christmas dinner or any special occasion.

Servings: 4

Total Time: 1hour

Ingredients:

- 7 ounces pearl barley
- Olive oil
- 2 William pears (halved, cored, cut into wedges)
- 1 tsp ground cinnamon
- 4 oven-ready partridges
- Salt and black pepper

Directions:

1. In a deep pot of salty water, cook the pearl barley for just under half an hour until tender. Drain well.

2. Preheat the main oven to 390 degrees F.

3. Warm 2 tbsp of olive oil in a pan over moderate heat. Add the pears and cook for 3-4 minutes until caramelized.

4. Transfer the pears to an ovenproof dish and sprinkle with cinnamon.

5. Using the same pan and 2 tsp more oil, brown the partridges until evenly golden all over.

6. Arrange the partridges on top of the pears and drizzle with a drop more oil. Season with salt and black pepper.

7. Leave the dish in the oven and cook for 20 minutes until the meat is cooked through. Let the meat rest for several minutes.

8. Slice each bird in half lengthways and serve with the pears.

Scandinavian Grouse Soup

Grouse is considered to be the king of feathered game. Using homemade stock is the difference between a good soup and a great soup! And this stock featuring allspice berries, juniper berries, ginger, and veggies makes all the difference.

Servings: 6

Total Time: 2hours 30mins

Ingredients:

Stock:

- 3 quarts water
- 1 tbsp salt
- 2 whole grouse
- 14 allspice berries (crushed)
- 14 juniper berries (crushed)
- 1 tbsp dried lovage
- 1" chunk fresh ginger (peeled and diced)
- 1 yellow onion (peeled and diced)
- ½ ounce dried mixed mushrooms
- ½ ounce dried porcini mushrooms
- 2 carrots (peeled and chopped)

Soup:

- 1 cup rye berries
- Salt
- 2 tbsp salted butter
- 1 yellow onion (peeled and sliced thinly)
- 1 carrot (peeled and sliced)
- 1 cup fresh peas
- 1½ tsp smoked salt

- Small handful fresh parsley (chopped)

Directions:

1. First, prepare the stock. Pour the water into a deep pot over moderate heat, season with 1 tbsp salt, and add the grouse. Bring to a simmer and then turn the heat down low so that the pot is steaming, not bubbling. Cook the grouse for half an hour before pulling them out.

2. Remove the breast meat from the birds before returning the remaining grouse to the pot, cook for another half an hour.

3. Once again, remove the birds from the pot and remove all remaining meat. Put the meat to one side for later. Return the bones to the pot. Cook for another 1-2 hours.

4. Add the berries, lovage, ginger, onion, mushrooms, and carrots to the stockpot and bring to a gentle simmer. Simmer for around an hour before turning off the heat.

5. Using a fine sieve lined with kitchen paper towel, strain the broth into a clean pot.

6. To make the soup, add the rye berries to a pot and cover with enough water to submerge the berries by 2" place over moderately high heat, season with a generous pinch of salt and boil until tender.

7. Place a second deep pot over moderately high heat and melt the butter. Add the onion and sauté for 3-5 minutes until softened.

8. Pour in the prepared stock along with the sliced carrots. Heat until steaming. The berries should have finished cooking at the same time as the carrot has become tender. Add the peas to the pot along with the cooked grouse and season with smoked salt, cook for 3-4 minutes.

9. Drain the rye berries and divide between bowls, ladle over the soup and garnish with fresh parsley before serving.

Wild Duck with Grapes in Red Wine

Wild duck with its rich, indulgent flavor is perfectly paired with sweet grapes and pearl onions and roasted in red wine for a delectable dish you won't forget!

Servings: 4

Total Time: 2hours 20mins

Ingredients:

- Salt
- 1 large wild duck
- 1 cup dry red wine
- 1 cup poultry stock
- 2 bay leaves
- 1 pound seedless red grapes (on the vine)
- 14 pearl onions
- 1 bunch fresh thyme

Directions:

1. Set the main oven to 400 degrees F.

2. Generously salt the duck inside and out.

3. Into the bottom of a Dutch oven, pour the red wine and poultry stock. Add the bay leaves.

4. Add the grapes, pearl onions, and fresh thyme to the Dutch oven and nestle the duck on top. Cover with a lid.

5. Arrange in the oven and roast for 1½ hours before removing the lid. Cook for approximately 20 minutes, until the skin crisps*.

6. Move the duck out from the oven and allow to rest for 5-10 minutes before slicing and serving alongside the cooking liquid and roasted grapes and onions.

*This may take up to 40 minutes depending on the size of the duck

Small Game

Armadillo in Mustard Sauce

Armadillo lovers say that its meat tastes like good quality pork. Apparently, it is a great alternative to chicken, pork, or beef in all sorts of dishes.

Servings: N/A*

Total Time: 9hours 25mins

Ingredients:

- 1¼ cups dry white wine
- ½ cup oil
- 2 garlic cloves (peeled, crushed)
- 1 armadillo (cleaned and cut portions)
- ¼ cup butter
- 1 medium-size onion (peeled, thinly sliced)
- Salt and pepper (to season)
- ½ tsp thyme
- ½ tsp rosemary
- 1 tbsp Dijon mustard
- 1 tbsp cornstarch
- 1¼ cups light cream
- Rice (to serve, optional)

Directions:

1. Combine the white wine, oil, and garlic to a large container. Add the armadillo and, while occasionally turning, marinate overnight.

2. Remove the armadillo from the marinade and set the marinade aside.

3. In a pan, melt the butter in a deep-sided skillet, add the onions and brown the portions of the armadillo.

4. Fill the marinade into the pan and bring to boil.

5. Stir in the seasoning (salt, pepper, thyme, rosemary) cover with a lid and simmer for 1-1¼ hours until tender.

6. Move the skillet from the heat and arrange the portions of armadillo on a warm plate.

7. In a bowl, combine the mustard with the cornstarch and light cream.

8. Return the pan to low heat and a little at a time, stir in the mustard mixture.

9. Continue to stir until hot and thickened, but not boiling.

10. Pour the sauce of the armadillo and serve with rice.

*Serving size will depend on the size of the armadillo

Beaver with Sour Cream

Just as Native Americans once enjoyed the flavor of beaver now, so can you!

Servings: 2-4

Total Time: 9hours 20mins

Ingredients:

- 1 (2-4 pound) beaver
- ½ cup flour
- 1 tsp salt
- ¼ tsp paprika
- Oil
- 1 onion (peeled, sliced)
- ½ tsp salt
- ½ cup water
- 1 cup sour cream

Directions:

1. Prepare the beaver: Clean the beaver and soak it overnight in a large container of salted water (1 tbsp: 1 quart water).

2. Drain before cutting the beaver up and rolling the meat in ½ cup flour, 1 teaspoon salt, and ¼ teaspoon of paprika.

3. Fry the beaver in a pan, in oil until browned.

4. Arrange the sliced onion over the beaver, to cover. Sprinkle with ½ teaspoon of salt.

5. Pour ½ cup of water over the beaver and cover the skillet with a tight-fitting lid.

6. Simmer for 45 minutes.

7. Add the sour cream and continue to simmer for 15 minutes.

8. Serve and enjoy.

Cornmeal-Fried Frog Legs

A southern delicacy these fried frog legs make a great appetizer or snack.

Servings: N/A*

Total Time: 8hours 15mins

Ingredients:

- Fresh frog legs (as required)
- Buttermilk (for marinade)
- 1 cup cornmeal
- ½ tsp salt
- ¼ tsp black pepper
- ¼ tsp cayenne
- Pinch of ground cloves
- Pinch of ground ginger

Directions:

1. Add the frog legs to a bowl and marinate overnight in the buttermilk.

2. In a bowl, combine the cornmeal with the salt, pepper, cayenne, cloves, and ground ginger.

3. Remove the frog legs from the bowl, shaking off any excess marinade.

4. Dredge the frog legs through the cornmeal mixture.

5. In small-size batches, fry at 325 degrees F, for approximately 6-8 minutes. It is important not to overcook the frog legs.

6. Serve with your favorite dip or ketchup.

*Servings will depend on how many frog legs you intend to cook

French-Style Wild Rabbit Casserole

One mouthful of this wild rabbit casserole featuring apple, cider, and tarragon will immediately transport you to the Normandy countryside.

Servings: 4

Total Time: 10hours 45mins

Ingredients:

- 7 ounces dried cannellini beans
- 7 ounces pancetta
- 4 tbsp of olive oil (divided)
- 2 large-size shallots (peeled, finely chopped)
- 2 dessert apples (peeled, cored, and diced)
- 2 tbsp flour
- Sea salt and black pepper
- 1 large wild rabbit (jointed into 8 pieces)
- 2 cups cider
- 1 bunch of tarragon (removed and chopped, divided)
- 1 bay leaf

Directions:

1. Overnight, soak the cannellini beans in cold unsalted water.

2. Drain and wash the soaked beans in the following day.

3. Put the beans in a large-size pan along with lots of cold unsalted water and simmer for 40-60 minutes, until cooked through. Drain beans and move them to a huge flameproof baking dish.

4. Preheat the main oven to 375 degrees F.

5. Over moderate heat, in a large skillet, fry the pancetta in 1 tablespoon of oil until golden. Use a slotted spoon and switch to the baking dish.

6. Reduce the heat and add a drop more oil to the pan.

7. Next, add the shallots and fry gently for 5 minutes before adding the diced apple. Cook for an additional 5 minutes and transfer to the baking dish.

8. Add the flour to a freezer bag and season liberally with salt and pepper.

9. Place the pieces of rabbit in the bag and shake to coat evenly.

10. Add an additional 1 tablespoonful of oil to the pan, and in batches, fry the rabbit until browned all over. Add the rabbit to the baking dish.

11. Using ½ a cup of cider deglaze the pan, scraping off any browned bits from the bottom of the pan. Transfer the mixture to the baking dish.

12. Pour the remaining cider into the baking dish and stir in half of the tarragon followed by the bay leaf.

13. Place the baking dish over moderate heat and bring to simmer.

14. Cover the pan and place it in the oven. Cook for 60 minutes, until the meat is bite-tender.

15. Taste, season, garnish with the remaining tarragon, and enjoy.

Frog Legs with Sauce Piquante

High in protein, potassium, and omega-3 fatty acids, frog legs should definitely be on the menu. Their taste is said to be very much like chicken crossed with fish.

Servings: 4

Total Time: 45mins

Ingredients:

- 2 tbsp canola oil
- 4 pairs large frog legs
- 2 tbsp all-purpose flour
- 1 cup onion (peeled, diced)
- ¼ cup green bell pepper (diced)
- ¼ cup celery (diced)
- 2 cloves garlic (peeled, minced)
- 1 tsp salt
- ¼ -½ tsp cayenne pepper
- 1 (28 ounce) can crushed tomatoes and liquid
- 2 cups seafood stock
- 1 tsp hot sauce
- ½ tsp dried thyme
- 1 fresh bay leaf
- 1 tbsp fresh parsley (chopped)
- 1 tsp freshly squeezed lemon juice
- Hot cooked rice
- Fresh parsley (chopped)

Directions:

1. Over moderate-high heat, in a large frying pan, heat the oil.

2. Add the frog legs and gently brown on both sides for approximately 10 minutes.

3. Transfer the frog legs to a serving platter and put to one side.

4. Add the flour to the pan and cook while constantly stirring for 4-5 minutes until a tan roux forms.

5. Next, add the onion along with the bell pepper, celery, garlic, salt, and cayenne and cook for 3-4 minutes, until wilted.

6. Add the tomato stock followed by the hot sauce, thyme, and bay leaf.

7. Once the mixture starts to simmer, turn the heat down to medium, while occasionally stirring.

8. Arrange the frog legs in the sauce, and cook for 8-10 minutes, while basting with the sauce.

9. Taste and adjust the seasoning, as required.

10. Stir in the chopped parsley and fresh lemon juice.

11. Remove and discard the bay leaf.

12. Serve with rice and garnish with chopped parsley.

Hare Braised in Red Wine

A hearty winter's meal, with all the flavor and intensity of spices and red wine. Enjoy with crust bread.

Servings: 8

Total Time: 14hours 50mins

Ingredients:

- 1 hare (washed and cut into 8 pieces)
- 1 tsp ground small game spices (any brand)
- Salt (to season)
- Black pepper (to season)
- Flour (as needed)
- 8 tbsp duck fat (divided)
- 2 cups poultry or chicken stock
- 2 cups small-size onions (peeled)
- 2 cups mushrooms
- 2 tbsp balsamic vinegar

Marinade:

- 2 cups red wine
- 1 onion (peeled, chopped)
- 1 carrot (chopped)
- 1 celery stalk (chopped)
- 1 tbsp small game spices (any brand)
- 2 tbsp wine vinegar
- 4 garlic cloves (peeled)
- Crusty bread (to serve)

Directions:

1. Add the hare along with the marinade ingredients (wine, onions, carrot, celery, spices, wine vinegar, and garlic) to a bowl. Cover the bowl and marinate for 12-48 hours.

2. Drain the hare and using kitchen paper towel, pat dry.

3. Season the meat with the spices, salt, and pepper. Roll each piece of meat in flour.

4. Over moderate heat, heat a heavy pan. Add half of the duck fat and brown the meat.

5. In the meantime, transfer the marinade ingredients in Step 1 to a large pan. Fill in the stock and bring to boil. Skim off any surface scum. Allow to simmer for 10-15 minutes.

6. Through a colander, drain the marinade.

7. Transfer the drained marinade to the pot holding the meat. Coat with a lid and simmer for 1-2 hours until the meat is very tender.

8. In a second pan, heat the remaining duck fat, add the onions along with the mushrooms.

9. Once the meat is tender, add mushrooms and onions along with the vinegar. Allow to simmer gently for half an hour.

10. Take out of the heat and set aside to rest for 30-40 minutes before serving.

Italian Rabbit Stew

This stew originates from the island of Ischia, which is just off the coast of Naples. Serve with new potatoes and seasonal veggies.

Servings: 6

Total Time: 1hours 10mins

Ingredients:

- 2 rabbits
- Salt and black pepper
- Flour (to dust)
- Olive oil
- 1 garlic bulb (cut in half)
- 10½ ounces shallots (sliced)
- 1 chili (cut in half lengthways)
- 2 cups white wine
- 7 ounces tomatoes
- 2 cups vegetable stock
- 2 bay leaves
- 1 bunch of basil (coarsely chopped)
- 1 bunch of parsley (coarsely chopped)
- Basil leaves (to garnish)
- 2 sprigs of rosemary (to garnish)

Directions:

1. First, join the rabbits into portions (shoulders, ribs, loins, and hind legs).

2. Season all portions of the rabbit with the salt and black pepper and lightly dust with flour.

3. Over high heat, in a frying pan, heat a drop of olive oil. Add the rabbit to the pan and sauté until golden brown. Put the rabbit aside and discard the olive oil from the pan.

4. Add some additional olive oil to the pan, along with the garlic, shallots, and chili. Cook for 2-3 minutes, until the shallots are golden.

5. Return the rabbit to the pan and using white wine, deglaze. After 5 minutes, add the tomatoes and pour in the vegetable stock.

6. Cook over moderate heat for approximately 20 minutes.

7. Add the bay leaves, basil, and parsley and continue cooking over high heat for half an hour, until a thick sauce-like consistency.

8. Garnish with basil leaves and rosemary.

9. Enjoy.

Potted Squirrel with Sourdough

Squirrel is a sustainable healthy meat. Its nutty flavor, thanks to a lifetime diet of walnuts, pecans, and almonds, means it has an overall pleasing flavor.

Servings: 4

Total Time: 1hour 30mins

Ingredients:

- 5¼ ounces smoked streaky bacon (cut into lardons)
- 2 grey squirrels (jointed into 6 pieces)
- 1 banana shallot (sliced)
- 1 celery stick (trimmed, sliced)
- 2 garlic cloves (peeled, finely chopped)
- 1 bay leaf
- 2 sprigs thyme
- 6 juniper berries
- Salt and black pepper
- 2 cups dry cider
- 1 cup unsalted butter (to clarify)
- Sourdough bread (to serve)
- Watercress (to serve)
- Olive oil (to drizzle)

Directions:

1. Arrange bacon in the bottom of a crockpot. Place the squirrel pieces on top followed by the shallot, celery, garlic, bay leaf, thyme, and juniper berries.

2. Season with some salt and pepper and pour over the cider.

3. On low, cook in the crockpot for 6-8 hours until the bacon is melted and the squirrel meat super-tender.

4. Allow to cool. Pour the stock through a sieve and set the liquid aside.

5. Add the squirrel and as much bacon as is possible to a mixing bowl.

6. Using clean hands, pick the meat off the squirrel making sure that no bones remain.

7. Once all the meat is removed, combine it with the bacon and using a fork, mash.

8. Transfer to a food blender/processor for a smooth consistency or for a more rustic texture, leave as it is. You can add a spoonful of leftover liquid to the mixture if it is too dry.

9. Spoon the mixture into 4 ramekins and set aside.

10. On the stovetop, in a pan, melt the unsalted butter, skimming off any surface foam, and allow the chalky deposits to fall to the bottom. The golden mixture in-between is the clarified butter.

11. Pour the clarified butter over the squirrel, leaving a thin layer, and place in the refrigerator to chill for 60 minutes.

12. When you ready to serve, remove the ramekins from the fridge and bring to room temperature.

13. To serve, toast the sourdough and drizzle the waters in olive oil. Arrange on a plate along with the potted squirrel.

Sardinian Hare Stew

Gamey hare, red wine vinegar, saffron, and capers come together to deliver flavor to a wholesome, hearty meal. Serve with couscous or crusty bread and enjoy.

Servings: 6

Total Time: 3hours

Ingredients:

- 1-2 hares or rabbits (cut into pieces)
- Salt (to season)
- 4 tbsp olive oil
- ¼ cup capers
- 1 cup hot water (for blooming)
- Large pinch of saffron
- 1 large-size onion (peeled, chopped)
- 15 garlic cloves (peeled, chopped)
- ¼ cup red wine vinegar
- ½ cup + ¼ cup parsley (chopped, divided)
- Couscous or bread (to serve)

Directions:

1. Season the pieces of hare with salt and put aside for half an hour at room temperature.

2. Add the olive oil to 12" Dutch oven, over moderate-high heat.

3. Pat the hare pieces dry, and in batches, brown in the Dutch oven. You may need to turn the heat down to moderate at this stage. Remove the browned pieces of hare to a bowl, while you repeat the process with the remaining meat. This step will take around half an hour.

4. In the meantime, chop half of the capers. Fill a cup measure with hot tap water.

5. In the palm of your hand, crush the saffron and scatter it into the hot water in the cup. Allow the saffron to soak and bloom while the hare browns.

6. Once the hare is all browned, take it out of the bowl. Add the onion and sauté until browned.

7. Next, add the garlic and cook for between 1-2 minutes.

8. Add the vinegar, whole and chopped capers, and ½ cup of parsley, while nestling the pieces of hair tightly into the pot. The liquid should come at least halfway up the sides of the hare pieces. If this is not the case, add additional water.

9. Cover tightly with a lid and gently simmer over low heat. Check the cooking process after 2½ hours or until the meat is falling easily off the bone. Once it is, pull the meat out and strip it away from the bone.

10. Return the hare to the pot along with the remaining ¼ cup of parsley and mix to combine.

11. Turn the heat off and cover for 5 minutes.

12. Serve the stew over couscous or with bread.

Squirrel Stew with Paprika and Wild Greens

This Portuguese inspired stew is super tasty. It's packed with lots of fresh ingredients and makes the perfect mid-week meal.

Servings: 8

Total Time: 2hours 20mins

Ingredients:

- 3 squirrels (cut into serving portions)
- Salt (to season)
- Flour (to dust)
- ⅓ cup olive oil
- 2 cups onion (peeled, sliced)
- 3 cloves of garlic (peeled, minced)
- 1 tbsp tomato paste
- 1 cup white wine
- ¼ cup cider vinegar
- 1 tsp oregano
- ½ tsp red pepper flakes
- 1 tbsp paprika
- 2-3 cups whole peeled tomatoes (torn into large-size pieces)
- Salt
- 1 pound smoked sausage (sliced into bite-sized pieces)
- 1 pound wild greens
- Freshly ground black pepper
- Chili (to season)
- Vinegar (to season)
- Crusty bread (to serve)

Directions:

1. Season the squirrel portions liberally with salt.

2. Dust the squirrel in flour.

3. In a 12" Dutch oven, warm the olive oil over moderate-high heat.

4. In batches, so not to overcrowd the Dutch oven brown the squirrel.

5. Transfer the browned squirrel to a chopping board while you cook the remaining pieces.

6. When all the meat is browned, remove them from the Dutch oven and add the onion.

7. Sauté the onion for 6-8 minutes, until it starts to brown.

8. Add the garlic and cook for an additional 60 seconds.

9. Next, apply the tomato paste and mix well to combine. Cook for 2-3 minutes while frequently stirring.

10. Stir in the wine, vinegar, and approximately 1 quart of water.

11. Add the oregano, red pepper flakes, and paprika followed by the torn tomatoes and finally the squirrels. Mix to combine and bring to simmer.

12. Season to taste with salt and gently cook for 90 minutes, or until the meat falls off the bone.

13. Take out the pieces of squirrel and pull away from the bones. This will make it easier to enjoy the meat. Return the meat to the pot.

14. Add the smoked sausage and wild greens and cook for 10 minutes, until the greens are cooked.

15. Season with salt, pepper, chili, and vinegar and serve with crusty bread.

Author's Afterthoughts

thank you

I would like to express my deepest thanks to you, the reader, for making this investment in one my books. I cherish the thought of bringing the love of cooking into your home.

With so much choice out there, I am grateful you decided to Purch this book and read it from beginning to end.

Please let me know by submitting an Amazon review if you enjoyed this book and found it contained valuable information to help you in your culinary endeavors. Please take a few minutes to express your opinion freely and honestly. This will help others make an informed decision on purchasing and provide me with valuable feedback.

Thank you for taking the time to review!

Christina Tosch

About the Author

Christina Tosch is a successful chef and renowned cookbook author from Long Grove, Illinois. She majored in Liberal Arts at Trinity International University and decided to pursue her passion of cooking when she applied to the world renowned Le Cordon Bleu culinary school in Paris, France. The school was lucky to recognize the immense talent of this chef and she excelled in her courses, particularly Haute Cuisine. This skill was recognized and rewarded by several highly regarded Chicago restaurants, where she was offered the prestigious position of head chef.

Christina and her family live in a spacious home in the Chicago area and she loves to grow her own vegetables and herbs in the garden she lovingly cultivates on her sprawling estate. Her and her husband have two beautiful children, 3 cats, 2 dogs and a parakeet they call Jasper. When Christina is not hard at work creating beautiful meals for Chicago's elite, she is hard at work writing engaging e-books of which she has sold over 1500.

Make sure to keep an eye out for her latest books that offer helpful tips, clear instructions and witty anecdotes that will bring a smile to your face as you read!

Printed in Great Britain
by Amazon